Hill, Harland A.

Cure your devotional blahs

CURE YOUR DEVOTIONAL BLAHS

Harland A. Hill

Published by

VICTOR BOOKS

a division of SP Publications, Inc.

WHEATON, ILLINOIS 60187

Scripture quotations in this book are from the King James Version unless otherwise indicated. Other versions quoted include the *New American Standard Bible* (NASB), © 1971 by the Lockman Foundation, La Habra, Calif.; and *The Amplified Bible* (AMP), © 1965 by Zondervan Publishing House, Grand Rapids, Mich.

ISBN 0-88207-600-0

Printed in the United States of America

VICTOR BOOKS
A division of SP Publications, Inc.
P.O. Box 1825 • Wheaton, Ill. 60187

[redacted]

CONTENTS

[redacted]

1
what's meant by devotions?

Simon laid down the heavy oar. For the first time he realized his softened hands were blistered. He was wet and cold, and every muscle ached. But it was good! Good to be back in a boat, to battle the nets, to shout in the dark, and again be a fisherman. And to top it off, a voice on the shore had told him and his fellow fishermen to cast on the *right* side of the boat—and they suddenly had the catch of their lives! Now, minutes later, a thin streak of early light began to spread in the east. Time to call it a night.

Simon didn't think of who the Person on shore was until John thumped his shoulder. "Look! It is the Lord!" Suddenly Simon recognized the familiar shape, the familiar lift and angle of His beard. And a knife seemed to twist within Simon. It *was* Jesus!

The heavy boat rocked with his leap, and Simon, strong man with a heavy heart, splashed urgently shoreward with frenzied arms. He reached shore only brief, panting moments ahead of the others.

"Come and eat." The voice was familiar, and

how it hurt. Simon picked up a short work-cloak to towel his hair and cover his wet skin. They ate quietly, seldom talking, Simon glancing away if their eyes chanced to meet.

Simon knew what he should say and tried hard to swallow a mouthful of soft meat. It wouldn't go past his dry, lumpy throat. Wouldn't go into his knotted, burning stomach. The man Simon who'd never backed down, never willingly admitted mistakes, and never saw himself clearly until the week before—Simon, the talker, searched for words that wouldn't come. Barnyard sounds drifted down the shore, and he heard a rooster greeting a new day.

"Simon, son of Jonas, do you love Me?" *His* voice. Strong and sure. The knife twisted again and Simon sighed, deep in his chest.

"Yes, Lord. You know I love You." He half muttered the words and He clenched his blistered hands.

"Feed My sheep."

The silence stretched.

"Do you really love Me, Simon?"

Simon burned a little inside. What did He want? "You know I do, Lord."

"Feed My lambs."

All was quiet again.

"Simon!" The voice held authority and Peter looked up, startled from his silence. "Do you, son of Jonas, really, truly, irrevocably love Me?" The deep eyes held Simon Peter's in a long steady look.

Peter stood up to shout, but the eyes held him. His voice caught suddenly in a burst of love, exasperation, and half-sob. "Lord, You *must* know I love You. You know everything!"

"Feed My sheep."

The two looked into each other's hearts. The dawn was as clear and bright as the air of heaven.

They understood each other and the world has not been the same since.

The full story is in John 21.

Such an intimate meeting should happen to each of us, you know—every day!

A quiet time in itself is not enough. It must be more than spending a few hurried minutes reading and praying. We need to meet with the Lord Himself, to tell Him of our deep love. When we bring our bruised selves to Christ, accept the truth that He knows our needs and how to heal us, and receive our commission for the day from His lips—then we have had true devotions.

2
God can make you tingle!

The night Paul and Silas sang so lustily to cause an earthquake, they weren't enjoying the comforts of Philippi Hilton. These two amazing Christians who scared the living night lights out of a Philippian jailor (Acts 16:25-30) were singing a duet deep down in the jailor's guest dungeon. Paul and Silas were locked in stocks, their feet chained, and the local rats squeaked, trying to throw them off pitch.

What made them sing, anyway? Who can sing in jail?

You enjoy singing in the shower. The hot needle-point action makes you tingle and you feel so good you want to sing. When Paul and Silas got to talking with God there in the dark of the dungeon, His answers and His presence made them tingle. God gave them a song. They had to sing.

God can make you tingle, too. He's not about to send you an earthquake (unless you need it, of course), but if you spend time with Him He'll certainly make you so glad you'll feel like singing, (see Ps. 98:1-2). It's Christ's personal suggestion that you take a little time for private devotions (Matt. 6:6-8), read the Scripture (John 5:39), ask for what you need (Matt. 7:7-8). No matter how often you're with God, His presence can make you tingle (Ps. 16:11). But you can only prove that by trying it. No one could love you more than God does or wish better for you (John 3:16).

How to Start

God never gets in a rut, so be prepared for the unexpected. In addition to your King James Version of the Bible, get hold of a version that talks your language; buy a paperback if you're short of cash. There are many good translations and paraphrases available, and they make God's thoughts easier to understand than at any time since Christ was here among His disciples. Compare your new version with King James—read from both.

Look for a thought that's new to you. God wants to help you find a verse, phrase, or challenge that's going to help you during the day. You will never run out of material, believe it or not. Read a paragraph at a time, a thought-provoking sentence, or even a whole chapter—not always a set number of verses. Read a whole book at one sitting once in a while. Follow a list of devotional readings or follow a plan of your own. Do what works for *you.* They're your devotions—and private—so be as independent of other people as you feel you must. Let God direct you.

Mull over your new thought during the day at odd moments, all day long; or all night long, if that's your shift. You'll tingle frequently, for these are God's thoughts for our modern world and He's personalizing them for you. Buckminster Fuller, one of today's best thinkers and a top-grade scientist, thinks through and rewords the Lord's Prayer *each night.* He's been doing it for years, he says, and he still tingles as God shows him new insights in the familiar words of the prayer Christ gave His disciples.

Just for You

God's Word–our New Testament, in particular–was written to get through to *you.* It's sharper, more penetrating than a modern electric needle designed to separate the tiny linings of the eye (see Heb. 4:12). That means when truth in our time is hard to separate from all the maybes and the "almost as goods," He'll help you find what you need.

The ads tell us there's a commercial breakfast juice with more zip and vitamins than you can get in natural fruit. It's used in space, yet! You need a zing of a special sort to start the day right, spiritually as well as physically. A physical zing wears off during the day, even in young people. But God's zing doesn't! It gets zingier, if anything, and it spreads and develops as God lays it on the line in your mind.

If a truth is new to you, it's as good as though it were invented for you personally. Even that most sophisticated of kings, Solomon, got excited enough about the new truths he "discovered" to write a book or two. So you can be forgiven for bubbling over on occasion and sharing your zing, your joy, and your experiences with others.

The late Sam Shoemaker, pastor and author, wrote about the special thrill or tingle he felt when God used him in a special way. He felt it *physically*–almost like an electric current. Many others have had this experience, although some of the best Christians never do. Some of us wouldn't know how to handle it. But, if you can handle the current, *God wants to communicate through you.*

When Christ worked a miracle in His ministry, people were amazed, excited, even frightened. He took advantage of these moments to establish truths. Can you imagine the thrill of being a disciple yourself? Of knowing that you're with the real, live, flesh and blood Christ? When He was on earth, His disciples literally and physically worshiped Him. It's safe to say that He excited them. He'll excite you too!

Emotions Aren't Devotions

Your adrenal glands are what some people call the fun glands—they help you feel excitement, thrill, and fear. But *they* don't bring you closer to God any more than does your sense of rhythm or harmony. All these can be a part of your religious experience, of course, and they often will be, but God is just as real to nonvibrators as He is to any of the turned-on generation.

He's not a cheap God, even though His gifts are free. If you're bored with God apart from your emotional highs, you should be careful that you're not worshiping someone's showmanship, your own glandular action, or, worst of all, a religion substitute supplied by the devil himself.

God Helps You Face Reality

Reality is what you have to live with, and it's the substitutes that offer escape, not God. Life has some hard-nosed and inescapable problems which your devotions will help you face and conquer with God's help. When you stop to think about it, Jesus Christ had His moments of wanting out, too.

His lonely prayer in Gethsemane sounds very much like some of our own: "Do I have to go through with this, Father?" (see Mark 14:32-36)

When God can't let us out, He'll help us through, just as He did His only begotten Son after He said, "Nevertheless, not what I will, but what You will."

Very few of us go through testing of such severity, perhaps none. Yet with faith in God and a dependence to match the situations we meet, we can do what's necessary for us, as God views it. Not on emotions alone, though. *You can build yourself up through daily devotions that are real and realistic* (see Matt. 17:20-21) *and be ready no matter what comes.*

Regular Station Stops for Faster Starts

A regular schedule of servicing works as well for Christians as it does for autos. God adjusts your valves, or something like that, when you read His Word and talk with Him. So, do it regularly.

The disciples talked with Christ, as they did with each other, and they did much of their learning while they walked from one place to another. Why shouldn't you? They learned to do what He wanted by taking instructions from Christ and then practicing in real life. You can, too. Paul wrote many letters, talked to many people about Christ, and as he wrote and talked, he learned from God. You will, too.

Peter insisted on sticking his neck out and was always impatient to get on with the job—or the comment. He made mistakes, but he learned from his mistakes, so you're in good company if you do the same thing.

As you make your devotional station stops, God will help you see more of His will, and you'll adjust with a great deal less shock than if you wait until you need a major overhaul because of neglect.

Stay Awake

Not many will admit it, but a lot of people fall asleep praying. So it's possible that a little discomfort might *help you pray* better. Prayer is essential! Christ needed it for Himself—often. And He recommended it many times to His followers.

Good prayer is private: "When you pray, enter your inner room" (Matt. 6:6, NASB). So find an effective way to take your inner room with you. Pastors pray while they're driving from one appointment to another (*most* of them keep their eyes open!). Housewives pray while they're doing housework and tending the kids. Astronauts pray while they're orbiting. And so on.

Moving around doesn't guarantee you're praying right though, even if you do stay awake. You can muddle things up whether you're vertical, horizontal, or bent, if you try hard enough. The old folks used to say, "An idle mind is the devil's workshop." Right! A mind running at idling speed or out of gear is a good staging area for little demons, too. So, be a genius; focus your mind!

When God wants to speak to you, tune in carefully. He may come on in bursts and want your undivided attention for several seconds or several minutes. Afterward you can mull it all over and decide what it means. And what to do about it. Or, God's Word may just *seep!* But He'll come through to you if you're willing to listen, that's for sure.

Turn up your hearing aid, for God seldom shouts. In the best verse on private devotions in the New Testament (Matt. 6:6, again), Christ suggests not only that you get away from distractions, but also that you concentrate on God.

To Tingle, A'ready!

God *can* make you tingle! If you can handle the current, He may use you to communicate Him to others. When Christ spoke to the lonely misfit woman at the historic well in Samaria, she was curious, at first, and then thirsty (John 4:5-42). His questions and answers were direct and penetrating. And Christ was so communicative that she got all excited and went off to round up her neighbors. That's really surprising when you realize that they probably weren't speaking to her.

And they were convinced, too. Her witness was effective and her happiness was clear and undiminished.

Now, that's tingling!

3
why bother, anyway?

Remember that corny old fellow you used to quote when you were a kid? Somebody's supposed to have stuck a gun in his ribs and said, "Give me your money or your life!"

"Take my life," he quavered. "I'm saving my money for my old age!"

Personal devotions are a little like the old fellow's money. You need them now, but they're for your old age, too—say, a thousand years from now. For the moment, they help you stay honest, earnest, and prepared for eternity.

They really help with *today's* problems—at least Christ thought they did. He prayed before hard tasks like choosing the disciples (Luke 6:12-13) and facing the crucifixion (Luke 22:39-46). And for some problems He recommended fasting as well (Matt. 17:21).

Our Christ was a great reader of Scripture, which is another good hint. He was so familiar with it that He could quote the Bible's most pertinent verses to fend off the devil (Matt. 4:3-10) or to answer critics (Luke 13:15-16; and others). *He* had to study for this just as we do (Luke 2:49), apparently. And He knew the Scriptures well enough to find relevant verses or passages for special occasions (Luke 4:16-21). So, it's more than just a good guess that He had regular devotional sessions, privately, just as His people are supposed to do. He certainly recommended the practice and guaranteed the results in Matthew 6:1-13.

Every Day?

Sometimes devotional periods seem to get in the way of what we want right now. Let's face it honestly, we're not all that pious by nature. But devotions are essential in the same way that food is essential. Even food's a bother, too, sometimes, but we manage to eat regularly—and some of us do a little munching on the side.

When Jesus talked with the woman at the well in Samaria, He'd had a long, hard walk, but He put spiritual need ahead of His physical need and *He ended up so refreshed He didn't want food!* (John 4:27-34) He put His spiritual side first because He wanted to. He felt better for doing it and so will you. Witnessing, healing, and praying were vital *re*creations for Christ; believe it or not, as a Christian you're put together the same way.

If the disciples neglected their moments with Christ (devotions), they goofed. Their problems after the crucifixion are examples (John 21:2-7). And when they seemed to be unhooked in general, it turns out that they hadn't been as close to the Master as they should have been (John 20:25; 21:12; Luke 24:21, 25-27). They quarrelled, sought preference, and even had to be lectured by Christ. Did you ever miss devotions and have a day like that?

Old Testament, Too

Talking with God was a two-way affair in Old Testament times, too. God began it Himself when He spent those cool and pleasant evenings with His unique "first team," our famous ancestors (Gen. 3:8). God *likes* fellowship with human beings of real character and individuality, such as Enoch, Abraham, Moses, David, Isaiah, and many others in the Old Testament. God's whole plan for mankind is designed to enable men to develop personal maturity, discernment, and high character—and become friends with God.

The sacrifices and prayers of the people of the Old Testament were the devotions of the early years of mankind, in part. God required them daily. Mankind hasn't changed much, yet, and neither has God.

God Talks to Listeners

God wants to converse with you! And the more mature you become as a Christian (Matt. 5:48), the more you'll enjoy talking to Him and listening for Him. He's the One who made you, so He made you capable of true fellowship with Himself. Being with God is a real pleasure, not a bore nor a chore.

God has used many people down through history to speak for Him, perhaps most dramatically at Pentecost (Acts 2). It's important to note that His servants heard from God while they were listening for His voice, waiting for His indications, and while their minds were open to Him. This was true not only throughout the Bible (prophets, priests, writers), but also in all of recorded history (Brother Lawrence, Martin Luther, your own pastor). He may not use you to change history as

He did the great key figures, but God wants to speak with you personally as often as possible.

God is not often dramatic. He comes on almost incognito, oftentimes. He speaks through the Bible; through a growing awareness in you of His will; by a "still, small voice" inside you; through other people; through your impressions, your recall, and your devotional detective work. He values and uses your devotional periods for your personal good, better understanding, and even the relief of your conscience, as well as for letting you know His will.

If salvation were invented by modern man, it'd have a printed circuit, a computer hook-up, chrome knobs, and time payments. And it would wear out. Unlike an earth-made device, your personal God-tuned receiving set improves with use. And the more *you* use it, the more *He* uses it.

So-o-o! What are you waiting for?

4
how to revitalize private devotions

Ever get so used to yourself you almost know what you're going to say next? When your spring runs down, you need a new push, a fresh impulse, or a rewind. Doing the same thing each day for your devotions can make them so routine they're—let's face it—blah!

So, try something new! Here's a whole grab-bag to work with. Don't get all eager and try everything at once, however. One or two at a time.

Your devotions can do lots of things for you. Those few moments can give you new information about God, or the Bible, or even other people that God loves besides you. Then, too, God wants to speak to you, make you more like Christ, reveal His will to you, and inspire you for the day. What a treat! You may get bored with yourself, but you won't with God—and that's a promise!

Most of us read the Bible and pray. And occasionally God breaks through our bubble of self-interest. Then we wish it would be like that every time. Perhaps, if you try different things, it will be. Stick with the Bible and prayer, but by all means add some variety to your daily devotional time.

Be Creative

Write out a thought-for-the-day, a prayer, or a whole devotional reading of your own. Compose an epigram or a poem. Write a letter to God.

Be Vocal

Read your Scripture aloud, in private. Paraphrase it for the deepest meaning you can find within it. Pray out loud; reword your prayer so that it's different and you'll have to think it through. Sing a hymn and think of its words. Call a friend and share your devotional thought of the day—your pastor just might be interested!

If You're on the Move

Pray for the ones you meet. Smile and beam God's love through your smile. Do a good turn for God as your devotional privilege. Make a sick call on a stranger, newcomer, or a shut-in and pray for them. Find an opening in your conversation to mention something God's done for you. Express your appreciation of a friend's Christianity, to him.

Be Loving

Reduce a flaw in yourself; reduce your aggravation of another's problem or personality. Love someone you don't like by praying for him with real concern. Pray that your love will begin to show where it can count for God. Forgive a wrong that really hurts (you may need to pray for extra help here). Use your spiritual muscle *more.*

Pastor and Church

Pray for God's solution to the problems in your

church; ask for ways that you can aid, help change to take place without friction, or even pull yourself out of the way of good change. Ask God to help your pastor in this day's tasks—calling, counseling, study, driving, family matters, church puzzlers, fatigue problems. Pray for his creative ministry in your church, that he'll benefit the whole community, including the strangers he meets and the businessmen and the executive-types who see him. Ask God to show you how a shortage problem in your program can be met. Maybe more teachers are needed, or possibly there is a space problem.

Celebrate

Tabulate each answer to any of your prayers; pray a "thank You" for each one. Buy an inspirational book or magazine for someone who might need it or one that *might* be read by a non-Christian, to leave in the self-service laundry.

Try New Ideas

Note unusual thoughts in all your devotional reading for later reference. Copy out special thoughts and pass them along to someone else. Buy an inexpensive book of religious quotes (bulletin board stuff, maybe) or maxims and take one a day for your own thinking and elaboration. Memorize Scripture verses from your church calendar or a soul-winning course. Read a chapter a day from good religious books, an article a day from religious magazines. Teach yourself *not* to duck when a truth hits you.

Learn About Yourself

Take notes on your pastor's sermons and apply a thought a day during each week. Choose religious art and find the deeper meanings by looking at it thoughtfully each day for a week. Poetry, too. Apply the things that Christ said as if He said them to you alone—Sermon on the Mount, parables, prayers, and so on. Join or start a small discussion group and help keep the discussions loving and immediate (as opposed to general and distant) in application.

Old Stand-bys

Look up vital words in a good Bible dictionary. Try a topical Bible or read a page or two from one of the Bible handbooks. Try a daily devotional book or brochure. Find a book that will give you help on studying the Psalms. In a Bible commentary, study a verse or two each day for information you never guessed existed. Buy a "sermon annual" at a bookstore and read it for good sermons, illustrations, new ideas.

Prayer Specials

Pray for your congressmen, president, state and local officials by name. Pray for the missionaries of your church and denomination. Pray for the other pastors and churches of your community. Pray for people in hospitals, in mental institutions, convalescent homes. Pray for the teaching staff of your local schools, your firemen and policemen. Pick a country a day from the world atlas and pray for its leaders. As you read the paper, pray for the trouble spots of the world. Pray for the lay-witness efforts of your community.

Seek God's Will

Learn to pray for God's will in your own life, *no matter what.* Seek for God's will in ecology, the course of world events, our country's economy, scientific and space developments, the religious direction of *all* churches, our elections, our morals, etc.

Way-Outers

Ask and discover why you were ripe for your most recent loss to the devil and ask God for grace and strength to apply the antidote He wants you to use. Compose a written sermon for yourself complete with texts that are constructively helpful, not just the ones that condemn. Accept a dare from God: judge or criticize only if you're willing to be judged or criticized on the same basis (Luke 6:37). Keep count of the times you really resisted the devil and make it your "thank you" list for bedtime. Objectively decide whether you've lived *for* God during your day and figure out a specific method or opportunity to improve tomorrow.

If all this discipline bothers you, consider the benefits: the reward of mounting approval from God as you improve, the self-improvement for its own sake, and the mounting accomplishments God will give you, plus His deeper friendship.

Devotions are excellent to wake you up and get you started on the right foot. You're never too young to begin! A time of prayer and letting God speak to you will help you quit growling at the dog, glaring unlovingly at loved ones, and grumbling over the burned toast. By the time the rest of the family and the folks at the office or wherever you work decide the change in you is for real, you'll be well on the way to starting a new habit of living for God's glory instead of your own.

Everything you pay for good devotions (time, money, effort, discipline) is worth your while. You *need* variety and change; God made you that way. Insist on variety for your special times with God and He will help you make progress. And the more He gets your personal attention, the more vital, creative, healing, and stimulating you'll become to others.

5
how to revitalize family devotions

"What would Jesus Christ have done if He'd had to feed and clothe a family of four or five, compete with the kids for the bathroom, and still make a decent living in today's rat race? Plus get along with my boss and keep my spouse happy?"

Those are fair questions. What He did was harder, but He left us answers that apply to us in today's set-up. And one thing's for sure, He'd have found time for worship with the family. His first priority was right relationship with the Father. He always made time to listen to God, even if He had to stay up late or get up early.

When Christ worshiped, prayed, or listened to God, He was getting the answers to His problems before they occurred. He stayed up all night before He chose His disciples, for instance. Our forefathers used to call this being "prayed up." There's no better way to get the answer to a problem at the moment of need than to go to the source of all wisdom ahead of the need. The secret is to build up your power supply! We learn our skills ahead of time, and we build our houses and take out our insurance policies well in advance.

Fitting family devotions into a busy household is *hard.* If it seems to be just a duty, it's even harder. But when you love your family and you love your God, the loves will supplement each other. "A family that prays together, stays together," is more than an old adage. A *family* will develop togetherness, not "apartheid."

If you've never tried family devotions before, you'll need ideas and suggestions. If you've tried them and they flopped, you'll need more ideas and suggestions plus some encouragement that it won't turn out the same as last time. So, draw up a chair and let's get on with it.

Family worship can be started and revitalized best by building in variety, freedom of thought, and openness; by adapting to each other, by sharing, and loving; through changing as often as God and your needs seem to indicate; and in knowing that the form and the place of worship together are always subordinate to the needs and urgencies of the family group. Don't get welded to a method, but change as needed and in the direction the family needs to go.

Use Materials You Like

Begin with a variety of Bible translations and paraphrases—King James and a couple of others. When you read a difficult passage in one, try another translation or paraphrase to dig out the meaning. In addition to Bibles, have other helpful literature at hand. Bible story books and other Christian literature for youngsters may be just as helpful to the adults of the family—especially if one age will take the time to explain thoughts to another, in either direction. Check your Christian bookstore for helpful books. Make use of Christian magazines and Sunday School papers for the various age groups in your family.

Variety in Getting Together

Listen to radio devotions as family members separately get ready for breakfast (got enough radios?) and then pray and discuss around the table. Hold devotions on wheels as you go shopping together, drive to Grandma's, go on a picnic, or bike, or walk. Or even go for a drive in order to get away together in private. Try no-chairs devotions by standing, sitting, or lolling. Get together under the stars or in the swimming pool for discussions and prayer.

Pray for Others

Ask God to use your family to pray for and win specific people you know. Don't forget to hold a quiet celebration when God answers. Pray for specific church problems each day for a week, asking God to use the family in finding answers or helping.

Separate, But Together

Go to separate rooms by ones or twos to read, think, and pray, and then convene a few minutes later for family prayer and the Lord's Prayer. Set a time during the day to think and pray together even though you're separated. Listen to the same Gospel broadcast, then pray for two minutes by prior agreement. Pray together separately on the way to school, the job, the market. Call up and pray together on the telephone once in a while.

Now and Then

Make an unbreakable appointment with the family

once or twice a week. Set aside a special mealtime for discussion, questions on ethics or religion, and close with prayer over dessert. If you're separated during the week, plan the weekend time to include discussion and prayer several times and save up questions and inspirational thoughts for it. Driving home from church is a good time to discuss, as we all know, but don't forget to pray, too.

Cater to the Kids

Put the kids in charge of family worship. They won't let you forget about it when the time comes! And let them approach you and God in the way they want to. Perhaps they will want to use worship time for Show 'n' Tell, bringing an object that has meaning and explaining it.

Brainstorm a family problem by accepting and writing down *every* suggestion offered, with no negative comments allowed. Kids' suggestions sometimes sound empty or silly, yet *any* suggestion can lead to other and better ones as everyone contributes and expands on what he hears.

Kids sometimes have a refreshing way of interpreting Scripture and adults can often learn much from their comments. So encourage them to be different. If you want to be refreshed and helped, God will use your kids to do it. And be sure the family sings together when they ask, or suggest it yourself.

Never Together?

Write out a devotional thought and clip it near a news item that's relevant, or print a family question or a prayer request on the margin of the newspaper. Nearly everyone reads the comics, so don't overlook that page. One of the comic characters may have something to say that'll add to or remind you of a spiritual thought. Use a family chalkboard or a bulletin board and have your family members contribute a thought each day. Agree that each member owes one 3″ x 5″ card's worth to the family worship each day.

Ask someone to be responsible for tape-recording a Scripture selection in the evening so that each one may play it back during the day, adding his own contribution at the end. Personal prayers are *good* family worship contributions for anyone to add.

Snatch-devotions are better than none. Quote your verse for the day to each other as you meet and pass in a hurry or when you say so-long for the day. Each one of us needs to hear about love (so does God), so include it in your comments.

Put a Christian calendar pad in the bathroom to be read and added to at leisure. Leave a devotional leaflet there, too, with the understanding that family members should mention prayer items or devotional thoughts in the margin, if they wish.

Be Unusual

Leave a pad and pencil, plus a Bible, on the breakfast table—any thought or prayer allowed—and use them in bedtime discussion and prayer.

Get a guest speaker for your family's enrichment.

Ask for "gold-mine" spiritual thoughts or experiences.

Try team-teaching at home as well as team-learning.

Try stand-up devotions: one minute of silent prayer with hands clasped, closing with the Lord's Prayer.

Conduct change-the-world devotions, based on Matthew 18:19-20.

Try prayer-chain devotions, each person taking a separate place and time to pray about particular problems that are familiar to all; sometimes you can promise to pray only within a certain period.

Write out a family devotion to help some other family or person and leave it in the Laundromat; include whatever you want to, beginning, "Whoever reads this, we love you and are praying for you."

Very Special

Make a family agreement to fast and pray for a special need. Get up 10 minutes early for bathrobe devotions. Set an extra chair in the family circle for God and include your Unseen Guest in discussion and prayer. Make posters for family reminders and helps. Expect and mention Christ's return often; use it (as Paul did) as a stimulant for Christian life. Try pen-pal devotions when the family is separated.

Incomplete Family?

Devotions for the benefit of the unwilling members are especially important. Grouchy? Mean? Stuck-up? Insecure? Pray for them with love, even though you pray alone, and expect God to do His office work in their hearts. Deaf? Unwilling? Disturbing? Let them know they're truly welcome to the worshiptime and also that they're included in your prayers whether they're present or not. Friendly pressure, love, understanding, and God's will make changes; pray for patience, too, and that *you* will accept God's means and methods. If only one of the family wants devotions, ask for help, in prayer, from God; share your problem with someone who will pray with you about it.

Dedicatedly Unique

Hold noisy devotions as you get ready to leave in the morning–sing, pray, discuss through the walls, laugh together. Hold a happy time together over success, answered prayer, near escape, or simple joy. Try "Quaker" devotions; sit together informally in prayer or quiet until moved to speak by the Holy Spirit. Eyes-closed discussions can be very different and helpful. Try devotions around a table over popcorn or a family treat, with no comments barred. Hold your devotions with another family; invite them to dinner or dessert. Thanksgiving or praise-God devotions are good for everyone, now and then. Try holding Christian holiday "specials." Or Christian TV program "specials."

6
family circle fun and informal devotions

Did you know popcorn is very high in spiritual protein? One of those pretty girls who isn't supposed to have (or need) brains popped out with a whole bunch of truth kernels she saw in popcorn, while she and her family popped and ate it. Why not? Truth is where you see it, so follow your nose. Do something different; get a lead from any place; listen to the kids; ask what grandma remembers. Jesus would have used popcorn just like He used wheat and wind. Why shouldn't you?

One family found some of God's truths hidden in the rug pattern they were sitting on. A boy who thought he was cynical got an important revelation from rotted grass and the reaching branches of trees. Families with little kids hold hands while they say grace. A couple I know think they invented hand-holding, so they do it everywhere, prayers included. Another family puts their hands on their Bible together as they talk to God. Some families will discuss any problem, anytime—personal or family—and they always use it as a bridge to prayer. They report on the answers, too, with thanks.

Good families are always in style. They offer refuge from competition, freedom from unfair criticism, a responsive and empathetic audience, honesty with love, and mutual respect. Bellying down on the living room rug will get your heads together in more ways than one. It's good family cement.

Each new family has to find out what it's like on its own. Those that become family circles pass on a precious, unmeasurable heritage of love, security, and stability. Familytime is when the Christian ethic comes clear and takes hold. Mom and Dad can make it happen.

Jesus was quick to point out that you can't hope for eternal life until you understand children. You won't understand the nature of belief, personal honesty, and ground-level confrontation until kids teach you. Your kids' attitudes and beliefs are the simple stuff from which real faith is made! Kids will stay that way until they're forced to change—they're the smart ones.

So, learn from the kids as you try some of the following ideas—more than 30 of them. They've been tested in family circles and found effective. They will expand your spiritual horizons as they refresh with their variety. They'll help reinforce your Christian teaching and family love. And they all start with your regular Bible readings or devotional booklet.

Mind Openers

Wha' Hoppened?

With a biblical incident or parable as a starter, let a family member retell it as it would have looked to him if he'd been involved or was an onlooker. What would he have said? What would he have done if he'd had the chance? How would he have retold it when he got home? What part of life does this remind him of, now? As he gets into the story, he's seeing what really happened.

Character Study

After the regular devotional reading, ask a volunteer to tell who that reading reminds him of, and why. Biblical characters can and do remind us of friends; devotional incidents remind us of concepts and people who embody them; or they may recall other Scripture. Here's a constructive way to relate what you see and know to spiritual ideas and to take note of character-building concepts.

Word Response

Spend a devotional session in drawing up a list of Bible terms all should know, like repent, Christian love, Second Coming. Keep the list open for new ones to be added later on. Occasionally, mention one of the words at worshiptime and ask each member to respond with his reaction (that is, give more than the word's meaning). You'll end up considering family problems, national politics, doubts, and so on. Each person should have a second chance in the same session so that he can summarize after he's heard what others say. His own summary will stick longer than anyone else's.

What Else?

Writers, artists, idea-men, and philosophers keep bombarding an idea or theme with questions over and over to find what else it means or can suggest. It's one way to get *all* that's there. It takes time and patience, but it's worthwhile and fruitful. So, take a Bible truth, or a passage, and bombard! You don't have to do it all at once; take some time one day and come back to it each day for a week or so. New material each time will help open ideas up and give you amazing insights. The best results will come after you're sure you've finished!

Expanders

Favorite Persons

Once in a while, when the devotional thought seems to suggest it, pick out or ask for a favorite character (relative, biblical person, acquaintance, someone from literature or history) and have each family member tell what that person has added to his life. Note what made that person like he was, too. You may want to make assignments.

Futuristic

Another way to expand the meaning of devotions is to project any verse, thought, or belief five or ten years into the future. What will that verse mean at the wedding of one of your youngsters, at graduation, after the death of a loved one, and so on. It'll be different for each one of the family group. Maybe it's a good way to work on growing up.

Invisible Verses

"Here's a verse we never talk about" or "I never thought about that verse this way" are good discussion starters at worship time. You'll get into background information, real meaning of Scripture, the way we grow into life and see new meanings as we change, and the wonder of how kids help adults grow up. Kids seem to have infrared vision when they're looking at Scripture!

Happenings

Does your family feel free to bring in an event

from any area of life and say that it's like this or that Scripture? The modern truth is happening around us all the time, since God is ever active. So we need to train ourselves to see it, see the Bible happening now, see God in action in the street and newspaper. Train yourself to see ideas as an artist trains himself to discern color everywhere he looks.

Varieties

Vocations

Pick a category (housewife, student, officeworker) and ask each family member to think of someone he knows in that category. Then consider the kinds of problems they face, and then give a Scripture verse or thought that has a special relationship to that person's daily life. The Apostle Paul's writings, for instance, already do this (Timothy was a student). Develop insight and empathy, as well as understanding of Scripture applications.

Oldies

Write and sing new words to any favorite tune. Settle on a Scripture thought to work around and throw in lines and words as a group. Then sing it together. Fitting all the words in properly isn't *too* important, you know. If it's real good, share it.

Gossip

Starting from a devotional reading or the thought for the day, go around the circle defining, elaborating, or illustrating the idea, each in his own way. Each one must repeat or summarize what the previous speaker said before adding his thought.

Good Humor, Man!

After finishing devotions, discuss its thought until

you agree on a definitely good-humored way of implementing your devotional nugget. Make it something each can do, if possible. Next day, or after each one tries it, get reports. Only good-humored reports are allowed and good-humored or interesting results. Save this for gloomy days, maybe.

Funnies

What If . . .

A major religious journal has a regular cartoon on the "What if (Paul or someone) had said this!" Your family will enjoy translating some of our "new ideals" into possible, if improbable, parallels with well-known Scriptures (Daniel and the new morality, for instance). A teenager will teach himself why character and right are so essential, if he has a chance. But each of us is sensitive on favorite subjects and family humor can become barbed without trying very hard, so go easy on the sarcasm, personal jibes, and criticism. But don't miss the fun.

Bible Humor

Ask now and then for contributions of humor found in the Bible. For example: "Sons of Thunder" was Jesus' own nickname for two of His favorite disciples who were impetuous and even blustery, now and then (Matt. 20:21-23); Jonah's ride in a great fish has a lot of humor in it, even while it teaches us about Christ's death and resurrection and God's power to direct and care for us; a lad's lunch offered to feed a multitude brings on a whimsical smile; and Jesus' reference to a camel going through a needle's eye was intentionally comic in the idiom of the day while it taught a valuable lesson about sin. There are other events that have humor in them, too, when taken in context. You won't always agree on what's funny, but having a look will widen your view of the Scriptures and add some realism that's not there unless you look for it.

Situation Comedy

After a hard situation has been resolved for some of the family or all of it, it may seem gruesome, childish, or even funny, when it was like life or death at the time. Maybe Dad turned the wrong way while taking up the offering; Mom fell on her nose on the lawn; one of the kids broke a leg just being silly; or a favorite pet died and the whole family had to hold a funeral for it. Give your family an opportunity to laugh at you and themselves now and then over what happened and how it turned out. Teenagers do this very well, by nature, and are the world's best clowns when they choose to be. It's a good way to keep your mental health and learn to adapt; it's a constructive way to look back.

Chuckles

Religious people as well as the Bible are targets for numerous jokes and quips which are genuinely funny and often merited. Make a point of collecting them and using them to illustrate devotions. Chuckles are good teaching devices, tension relievers, and discussion starters. Because they're jokes and have a point, they will emphasize some strength or weakness of religious thinking or doing. Easy to listen to in small quantities, they'll spark a boring subject and even an atheist will be glad to help you collect them. Laugh at yourself and help the family! For example, each of us gets stuffy about our own point of view, occasionally, so look up what Paul says in Romans 12:3 on *that*. TV comics and cartoons in magazines portray preachers as straightlaced and stuffy, and religious people as intolerant and lime-light seekers; both accusations are true and a family is helped when it can see why such pretenses turn people away from Christ—who exhibited exquisite tolerance, openness, *un*stuffiness, and real love even when He was criticized.

Punch Lines

"A Strange Thing Happened!"
Use this old bromide to introduce a joke on yourself, on the family, an unexpected way God worked for you, or used you. Punch lines aren't always funny, but they can bring a group to attention. And the strange-things category includes miracles, embarrassments, triumphs, accolades, flubs, and even failures. ("A strange thing happened! I was *early* for Sunday School and I discovered the teacher goes half an hour early just to put things in good shape and to talk to anyone who wants to talk. Boy, did we talk!" Or, "How about that? I won. All that extra work Mom made me do must have done me some good.")

Far Out!
As every parent learns, humor is often the unexpected thing without intention of clowning. What are the far-out, unexpected thoughts the family gets during the Scripture reading? Daydreaming kids can lead to leaps of insight simply because daydreams do have a little bit of relation to what's going on. If it's amazing, fantastic, or something strictly out of the blue, it may still suggest truth no adult would reach by logic. Encourage everyone to share his mental wanderings. For instance:

"Where are you now, Johnnie?" "Can you remember what got your attention away from the reading? Your chain of thought in getting where you went? . . . Good! That shows you've got an active mind; good thinking." Or, if he's too far out: "Up to a point, that's helpful. Where do *you* think you got off the subject?" Too much daydreaming and wool-gathering can lead to trouble; and so can too little.

Jokers

If you're TV watchers, try relating and comparing the jokes, situation comedy, talk-show gags, and so on to Scripture and your daily life. Comedy that holds appeal for a mass audience has to be related to living, of course. (Situation comedy is based on normal living that goes wrong through mistakes or misunderstandings. Are drunks really funny? Is lying really something to laugh at?) This will go best if there's some understanding about when's OK to interrupt; it shouldn't interfere with everyone's enjoyment. Make the point again at worship time, too. Comedians aren't preachers, exactly, but they have to hit close to make a living.

Booby Hatching

There are enough booby-moments (people's stupid mistakes) in the Bible to give a booby-hunter a good time. Anyone who misapplies truth to make a ridiculous halftruth is a qualified, up-to-date booby, so you'll likely find one or two who sleep in your bed. Or check on Adam and Eve (Gen. 3:1-6), David (2 Sam. 11:2-17), Peter (John 13:5-9), and others in the Bible. Seeing boobisms while you're young is a way of reducing them when you're older–if you stay honest.

Games

Dishpan Devotions

When Mom's tired or needs a change of pace, try giving her some company and save her some work. The dishwasher quotes a verse as he washes a dish; the one he hands it to must wipe the dish until he can give an experience where the verse applied, his own personal thought on the deeper meaning of the verse, or another verse that carries on its meaning. This may slow down the wiping job, but those dishes will come out *shiny!* So will you!

Manna

Using a set of cards with printed Scripture verses (Scripture manna), let each family member pick a verse and then act out the meaning of his verse. After the family has guessed what the verse is, he may want to give his testimony to the family of what Christ meant to him yesterday.

A variation: Each person selects a familiar verse and spends a couple of minutes thinking about it. Each then restates the verse or talks about its meaning without quoting any part of the verse. The object is to guess the verse in each instance—and to profit from its message!

Another idea: After selecting verses, spend a minute thinking about them. Then have each person preach a two-minute sermon on his verse.

Guess-a-verse

Describe a circumstance where you think a particular Scripture applies. Give about two sentences to begin with; then add details as necessary until someone guesses the verse. (First hint: "I have this 'friend' at school who keeps threatening me with a punching when I won't give him the answers in class." Second hint: "Maybe he's not really an enemy, but he acts like one." Third hint: "So, maybe I should love him anyway, but I'm not so sure I do." Verse: "Love your enemies, bless them that curse you, do good to those that hate you, and pray for them which despitefully use you, and persecute you" (Matt. 5:44). If the "owner" must go beyond three or four hints, let him wait until next time around to reveal it. This will give everyone a chance to think more about it or look it up, of course.

Touchstones

After reading your devotional portion, ask someone (a hesitant type, maybe) to choose what he feels is a key word, short phrase, or the theme from the day's devotions. After some time for thought, let each one of the group supply his own meaning for it in the "Happiness is . . ." style ("Devotions is . . . ," for instance). Doing it well and keeping it short is good training for word use, thought discipline, and it's particularly excellent for future preachers or writers.

Buzzing

Use the old educational gimmick of buzz-grouping by turning the family into small groups to discuss nose-to-nose the meaning of a difficult Bible passage or question. Each group should write its findings and compare them in general session. What's the meaning of the passage for this family for this day? What are the special meanings for Dad, Mom, the kids? What's below the surface of the verse? What omission does it point out? What new approaches to old problems? How are you likely to bend it or twist this portion of the Bible as you apply it?

Holy Angles

Sparkers

When your devotions suggest it, ask questions. What would Jesus have done if He'd gone shopping in one of today's supermarkets? If He worked in your office or your job? If He went with your family to the football game, your last party, or to your church? Ask realistic questions and be realistic with answers. Jesus isn't difficult to predict when you know He served God totally, for God's glory. What's realistic religion in God's view? Certainly not any of that pie-in-the-sky routine! What does Paul say concerning the same questions?

Deep Thoughts

If you're reading in the Gospels, try stimulating the family curiosity by turning them loose on: What did Jesus believe that we don't? You'll get a zillion unexpected answers. Why did He do the *little* acts that are reported to us? What is He really saying? What promises did He depend on that we forget? Try to keep from being negative about the answers, here; that's not easy when favorite subjects are broken open!

Bugs

There are questions that don't get asked even in the best regulated families. Bringing up the topic "Are these sins covered in the Bible?" may help make your worshiptime an easy spot to bring up and discuss the questions that really bug your loved ones. "What's not mentioned in Scripture?" is another approach. "What should a Christian from this family do on a date?" "If the parents in this family went to the school the kids do, what would they have done at the same age?" Free discussion and self-determination go well together.

Thanks a Lot!
If it's routine to count blessings, ask some questions about appreciation. What am I thankful for: That I know you know? That I've never mentioned until now? That doesn't include food or money? That I thought of while I should have been listening to the sermon? That no one else in the world has? That's mine because I'm in this family? That's available because I'm a Christian? That I thought about while I was going to sleep? That I don't have and I'm glad I don't?

Mini-Sermon
Have each person select an object in the room and use it as the basis for a sermon or object lesson. You might select the telephone and talk about prayer. Or a clock and talk about valuable use of time. Or a light and talk about the source of power. Look around. There are countless things in any room that can get you started. Those participating should go to the Bible for Scriptures to relate to their mini-messages.

Follow-Ups

Discoveries
Report times on personal insights and experiences may go better if they're voluntary or else the whole family circle reports in the same session. "What I discovered since yesterday's devotions" is a good topic to involve the reporter (and a good teaching

technique). Assigning a reasonable Scripture research or learning task with the responsibility of reporting on it helps young and old respond more adequately. Like rationing of fuel, you perform better if you have a stake in the answer. "Show 'n' Tell" is good for reporting, too.

Hot Sermons

Take separate notes on the Sunday morning sermon once in a while and compare them during devotional time. Look up and read the Scripture, bring out the good points, note good quotes, disagree, and then enjoy yourself by saying the things the pastor left out (kindly, of course). You will be surprised at how much you'll all turn up. Your pastor might, too.

Devotional Ecology

Recycle a good devotional thought once in a while. Let anyone introduce one that made a big impact on him at the time he first heard it. After he tells about it, review what each remembers, what you've learned on the subject since, what you'd now like to add or subtract (you'll nearly always add). Children like to do this at all stages of their growing and their memories will surprise everyone. Aside from the memory exercise, it's good for articulating beliefs and forming concrete opinions.

Hiding the Word

Spend time after dinner two or three times a week memorizing the Word. Enroll in a contest sponsored by Bible Memory Association, P.O. Box 12,000, St. Louis, Mo. 63112. Or use some other course of Bible memory selections. Even Sunday School lessons prescribe certain memory work.

7

party devotions for fun

One of the best party "tricks" ever put on—if you'll excuse the language—was the turning of water into wine. Jesus Christ did it at a wedding. He did it to keep the party going and because His mother, good neighbor that she was, insisted on it (John 2:1-10). This indicates, among other things, that parties are important enough in the sight of God to merit His approval and blessing.

Today's vital Christian likes to go to parties, too, and he likes to get his time's worth all the way from the doorbell button to "Boy-I'm-full-good-night!" That should include the devotions which sometimes get left out because they don't seem to go with the rest of the fun and games.

Successful parties, as everyone knows, are lively, interesting, and noisy. If you have fringe benefits like young hearts and deaf neighbors, all the better.

Christ felt at home at parties, so if you want to keep up with God, you'd better believe you can have lively, interesting party devotions that'll plant good thoughts for later reflection. On the slim chance that you don't have anything like this lined up for your next bash, here are six varied suggestions that are mostly new. You'll need a minimum of props, a lively group, and some home-grown noise. Answers for each of the teasers are given at the close of this chapter.

1. *Hot-line* (scratch paper, newsprint, black marker, Bibles).

a. Draw a telephone dial so that everyone can see the letters and numbers in their proper relationship. Like this, for instance:

	ABC	DEF	GHI	JKL	MNO	PRS	TUV	WXY	
1	2	3	4	5	6	7	8	9	0

In addition to this, you'll need to list the hot-line numbers separately, along with Bible references as clues.

b. Put down the first hot-line number and then explain it.

c. Using the telephone dial as your decoding device and the hot-line numbers as the code, figure out the Bible message. For example, using the number 968 273 4373 and matching each number against the code-device or dial, you can get the words "you are here," though this is not a Bible message. Decode these:

A. 463 547 8367 (2 Chronicles 7:14)
B. 968 273 7368 (Matthew 28:19)
C. 437 773 7368 (John 15:23)
D. 232 948 6377 (Mark 5:19)
E. 537 877 2837 (Hebrews 7:25)

2. *More Truth than Poetry* (newsprint, scratch paper, Bibles).

When you get started on limericks, it's fun to keep right on going from one to another, corny or not. They're great in an open group with spoken or shouted responses.

Read out the Scripture references needed for the limerick coming up so they can be looked up while you're writing out the verse on the newsprint, leaving the last line blank. Make sure everyone knows that the Scripture holds a hint for a possible last line.

And have fun! These are great truths in clown's clothing, maybe, but that won't hurt or diminish them. You're bound to get as good or better responses from your group, so hold off with the final line given here until the group has had a good go. Then go on to the next. Folks may want to copy these things to use at Aunt Minnie's Lemonade Mix —why not?

a. Put a sign on the straight, narrow gate:
"Don't gamble on eternal fate!
To be sure you get in
Let Christ forgive sin—

____

(Matt. 7:14; Ps. 107:6-7)

b. There was a free-thinker named Jim
Who prayed loud and clear and with vim,
"Dear Lord, You can save me,
But don't rearrange me!"

____

(Matt. 18:26a, Ps. 51:10)

c. There is a weight-lifter named Faber
Who's vigorously opposed to his neighbor!
Now, God helps you love,
But not kick and shove,

____

(Rom. 13:9; Luke 10:36-37)

d. Got a problem with routine devotions
That affect nothing more than emotions?
You can fix that mistake
And give God a break

____

(Heb. 5:12; Matt. 22:29)

e. There was a young pastor named Shnook
Whose sermons, while not out of crook,
Showed mainly a knowledge
Of things learned in college

____

(2 Tim. 2:15; Ps. 94:12)

f. Pretty Eve didn't worry about wrong
When she heard the serpent's sweet song,
So, she just took a bite
For the apple looked right

____

(Gen. 3:23; 2 Cor. 11:3)

g. We're doing what anyone would
By returning good deeds for good;
But good deeds for bad
Are what make God glad,

____

(Titus 3:8; Luke 6:31)

h. Whenever you're troubled and tempted
To think all the fun's been preempted,
Hang in there, my friend,
We're judged at the end,

____

(Gal. 6:4, 7; 1 Peter 4:18)

3. *Pun-fun* (scratch paper for those who want to copy it and do it by themselves; Bibles and newsprint or chalkboard to print the game on for everyone to see.)

Puns aren't everyone's favorite word game, but they can sometimes point up Scripture truths. Here is a rare eight-item pun on one phrase, each suggesting a nugget of truth implied in the passages of Scripture. Match them up by drawing lines to the right one.

a. Genesis 4:3-5	The Son's inn site
b. Genesis 37:18-20, 25, 27	The son since sight
c. Genesis 37:22	The sons incite
d. Luke 2:7	The sons in sight
e. Luke 15:17	The Son's in sight!
f. John 9:17	The Son's insight
g. Matthew 9:4; Mark 7:21	The sons' sin site
h. Revelation 22:3-5	The son's sin sight

4. *ThingamaScriptures* (household objects, Bibles) Everyone knows that a mustard seed signifies faith (Luke 17:6). So what about all the other objects associated with scriptural teachings? Choose up sides, time the responses, and see who comes out ahead. Some of the objects are farfetched to add some difficulty and spice to the game. Correct response in 5 seconds gets 3 points; 10 seconds, 2 points; 15 seconds or more, 1 point. There are several possible responses, usually, depending on how difficult you want your game to be. If your group is pretty sharp, make them come up with the answers listed here. Answers are included here for playing convenience, this time.

1. Broom	Luke 15:8-10	Joy over saved sinners
2. Measuring cup	Matthew 7:2	The measure you give is the measure you get

3. Lamp	Matthew 5:16	Live to glorify God
4. A pearl	Matthew 13:46	Kingdom of heaven
5. Bread	John 6:35	Christ the Bread of life
6. Stone	John 8:7	Forgiveness
7. Cup of water	Mark 9:41	Service for God
8. Penny	Luke 21:2	Giving to God what counts
9. Bushel	Luke 11:33	Use talents for God
10. Seeds	Mark 4:3-8	Christian growth
11. Dime	Luke 11:42	Tithing, a minimum gift
12. Small child	Matthew 18:3-4	Childlike trust required
13. Doll or idol	1 John 5:21	Don't worship idols
14. Wheat grains	Mark 2:23-28	Sabbath freedom and its real purpose
15. Yeast	Matthew 16:12	Guard against false teaching
16. Bible	Hebrews 4:12	Power of God's Word
17. Bent straw	Matthew 12:20	Meekness of Christ
18. White stone	Revelation 2:17	Reward in the hereafter
19. Biscuit	Matthew 15:33-36	God's concern for our physical needs
20. Match	James 3:6	Damage done by the tongue
21. Piece of wood	1 Corinthians 3:12	Deeds that will be burned in God's fire
22. Salt	Mark 9:50	Vital Christianity
23. Sand	Matthew 7:26	Unwise builder in life
24. Mouth organ	Matthew 11:17	World leaders are like children
25. Twig	John 15:5	Union with Christ; we bear fruit only through Him
26. Napkin	John 20:7	Resurrection of Christ

27. Band-aid	Luke 10:33-36	Christian neighborliness
28. Rope or string	Matthew 22:13	Punishment for sin
29. Calendar	Mark 13:33	Second coming of Christ
30. Sheet	Luke 17:34	Be prepared for Christ's return

5. *Charades*

Charades, an old-time game, is still popular with many party groups, but it's surprising how seldom it's used with church groups. Use the regular rules and some characteristic group of biblical themes, such as aphorisms of the New Testament. Try these and have fun:

a. A city set on a hill cannot be hid.
b. Don't hide your light under a bushel.
c. Be sure your sins will find you out.
d. Love is the fufilling of the law.
e. You should return good for evil.
f. You're going to reap just what you sow.
g. The wise man builds his house on a rock.
h. If the salt loses its saltness, how can it be salty?
i. Give to Caesar the things which are Caesar's and to God the things which are God's.
j. Do unto others as you would have them do unto you.

6. *Alliteration* (newsprint, marker)

Compose, as a whole group, a 50-word-or-more statement of some aspect of your Christian belief or conduct with as many words as possible beginning with the same sound or letter. It should be written out in its complete and corrected form so everyone can see it clearly when it's done.

Give each one who wishes (or can be persuaded) a chance to say it moderately fast. The faster the better. The one making the least number of discernible slips is the winner, provided it's fast enough to qualify.

This is an excellent practice for tongue control (see James 3:5-8) and it is a standard training device for professional broadcasters and public speakers.

For example: Salvation is a sensible and salutary, yet spectacularly successful, solution to such sicknesses of the century as the salacious and sedentary slips of suburban circles, synergistic and semantic eccentricities, self-serving pseudosciences, and such subtle sins of our self-centered citizens as may sap the sufficiencies of the saint as well as the sinner. So seek the Savior's certainties and accept the sacrifice of the Son for yourself.

See? Nothing to it!

ANSWERS:

1. *Hot-line*
   - A. God listens
   - B. You are sent
   - C. He's present
   - D. Be a witness
   - E. Jesus saves

2. *More Truth than Poetry*
   - a. Then simply turn right and go straight.
   - b. I hope God was patient with him!
   - c. And it makes confrontation less labor.
   - d. So, go through His Book—not through motions.
   - e. And not very much from God's Book.
   - f. And Adam went meekly along.
   - g. At least that's what Paul understood.
   - h. And only the Christian is exempted.

3. *Pun-fun*

a. Genesis 4:3-5	a. The sons in sight
b. Genesis 37:18-20, 25, 27	b. The sons incite
c. Genesis 37:22	c. The sons' sin site
d. Luke 2:7	d. The Son's inn site
e. Luke 15:17	e. The son's sin sight
f. John 9:17	f. The son since sight
g. Matthew 9:4; Mark 7:21	g. The Son's insight
h. Revelation 22:3-5	h. The Son's in sight!

8
after devotions, what?

As soon as the sun comes up, roosters, alarm clocks, and little children are wide awake, noisy, and full of vigor. Bully for them! The rest of us need some time to face the dazzle and get our corpuscles on their way.

Still, it's a good idea to have devotions early in the day—as soon as you can focus properly. And after devotions, the fun begins!

After you've spoken with God, you have within you something like a timed-release knowledge pill. God puts it there within you if you let Him. Then God adds to the thoughts He's planted, and they expand, during the day, whether you're paying strict attention or not. You can't spend your time just mulling over ideas, of course, but there are moments in every job and occupation, every single day, when your mind isn't running at full intensity. This can be when the insights set in. "Aha! Why didn't I think of that before?" should be a daily and natural question.

The Apostle Paul *walked* many hundreds of sweaty miles cross-country during his missionary journeys. Guess what he thought about besides mosquitoes! It's more than likely that the deep teachings of his New Testament epistles matured during those journeys because his mind was in an accepting mood toward God. Even a saint can scratch and think at the same time! Or shave! Or wash dishes!

Use 'em

Use your devotions all day! Ask God to saturate your mind with His ideas and let them soak in as He does so. Implement them. Discuss them. Pass them along. Question them seriously to be sure they came from God and that you understand them. Relate them to your concept of faith. Reassess them. And maybe by the end of the day you'll get to the point where you *believe* what God's been trying to tell you. This is how most of us learn. And it won't take long to get into the habit of listening for God, at this rate.

Find ways to apply them. Just because some jobs lack a built-in schedule, they're a little harder and take more concentration and decision-making. Some jobs are so skitter-scattered you don't know what's on the up-take at the next crack in the pavement. And some jobs are mostly reflex, automatic. In each case, a Christian can use moments and opportunities as they occur to practice and establish God's thoughts with God-approved habits.

Any new habit can be learned quickly by applying it right away and at each opportunity. God made you that way, so that you could learn His will and apply His method readily, as soon as you see it.

Your motive is important to God. He "measures us around the heart." So steep your mind, reactions, *and motives* in God's desires for you. Fortunately you can do *all* these things while going about your duties. Paul says it well: "Do all things through Him" (Phil. 4:13, NASB).

There are uncounted benefits. Immediate, personal, and eternal benefits. Among them are the higher personal standard you're aiming for as a Christian, the sharpened skills of mental and spiritual discipline, an improved and focused thought-chain rather than those random dream-concepts that can go wild and make trouble. And as you work on these new ideas and habits, you become more like Christ. How about *that!*

Accept the challenges—they're your opportunities. When a ball-player goes on the field, he responds to opportunity according to his ability, his diligence in practice, his motivation for success, *and his inspiration.* We've seen these talented men perform with skill on TV and all these factors made a difference (don't think TV isn't a part of their inspiration!). Often *their first move is vital,* even though it's a small one. A brilliant play is pulled off by inches, but seldom is it done without strong motivation and positive reactions.

Your small decisions may be the important ones. It's hard to retract that first impulse, the first move. You may not be on TV, but the subtle temptation, the dull routine, or some completely unexpected suggestion are opportunities for brilliance. They're in your life-style and your reactions *are* your life-style. If the *devil's* throwing something at you, *right* impulses are the ones that count.

Christ exhibited a constant awareness of God. Not a bad idea!

Renew your commitment in action each time you see a chance. "Renew" is different from "parade." Practice right principle against impulse and even against inclination. Grant a hard forgiveness, unasked. Prick your smugness balloon. *You* can find ways to renew.

Your spring will run down, of course, sometimes. Devotions help us, but they're not enough. Christ made a practice of praying, then acting. This is the "after devotions, what!"

Don't think the devil stays licked! If you can be as persistently *for* God as the devil is *against* Him, you've got a great chance for success in Christian living.

And, when you goof, claim God's help and forgiveness right away (1 John 1:9–2:1).

9
how to lick the devil

None of us are likely to set aside 40 days and go into a desert retreat to prove we can lick the devil, with or without food. We're too busy, as well as too insecure (scared?); God doesn't ask it of us.

It's hard enough to lick the devil on the job, at home, in school, and on the street. But *if* you love God and *if* you want to lick the devil, you can do it as Christ so adequately proved and stated.

You don't have much privacy from the devil. He's well informed, he seems to have all the help he needs, and he's got this nasty trick of knowing your weak spot for the day. His favorite expression is "Gotcha!" and he'll often say it when you think, for once, you've got him licked.

Mr. Practical of the New Testament (James) gives us a strong verse to reassure ourselves when we need it: "Submit therefore to God. Resist the devil and he will flee from you. Draw near to God and He will draw near to you" (James 4:7, 8, NASB). Sure sounds easy, huh?

But life's peaks and puddles are unexpected and you don't always recognize the devil's ambush. And you get lulled into letting up. And life gets to seem so unfair. And the temptations are so provocative. So, *how* do you lick the devil?

Mind Set

Expect your temptations to be very appealing, of course. Make up your mind to "go with God." Try harder, too, for that's what the devil does; it fails, sometimes, but don't quit trying on that account. Try harder in the direction God wants next time.

Quote Scripture

Shoot Scripture bullets at the devil as Christ did (Luke 4:1-14). Throw Scripture at yourself as a devotional aid and reminder. Ask a friend for a verse that might help. Look up Ephesians 6:16 and put on your armor, as suggested; there are effective mental ways to put that armor on, so use them. Try a psalm-prayer of David's, like Psalm 51. Recall a sermon or a Sunday School lesson that helped you; ask God to help you apply it. Open your Bible where you are and read it thoughtfully, if you can.

Challenge the Devil

After you see your temptation for what it is, find a better way to say what you said, if it's already out, or hold your tongue until you can say it as God wants. Ask the visible tempter—boy or girlfriend, colleague, boss, spouse, kids—to reconsider. Figure out a way to be helpful to the one who's the agent of temptation. Take a deep breath and apologize; admit you're wrong and ask God for special help. Make the devil prove his idea is better than God's (careful, here; God looks at the long-run and eternal results). Pray for your visible tempter who's being used for evil purpose and may not know it at all.

Lean on God

Ask for God's specific help; ask what He wants you to do—and listen. Ask for His alternative (1 Cor. 10:13). What does God think about this? Give the Holy Spirit who dwells in you a chance to prompt and strengthen you. Hold a very private service to recommit yourself to God.

Lean Against the Devil

Rate your temptation (like they rate earthquakes) from one to ten; then it gets put in its place and you can handle it better. Decide why you're vulnerable today and work on the weak spot first; pray about it later, too. Ask seriously what's to be done if you weaken and give in and everyone finds out about it (they're likely to!). Find out why you're being attacked, from the devil's viewpoint; what's his attitude, and what's the advantage to him.

Attack!

Say no loudly and clearly and move to something else. Turn off the TV, get rid of the book, burn the magazine, label the porno or the oddsheet as pollution, in large black letters with a felt pen. Look somewhere else that's less tempting. Move away physically and mentally from the warmth or the immediacy of the person involved. Add up the faith you've prayed for at various times, know that it's available to you, and *use it* as an act of collaboration with God. Give in to God's will, *now!* Go as far as you can see in the right direction, even if it's only an inch or so.

Get Help

Ask the advice of a doctor, lawyer, trusted friend, counselor, or pastor; sometimes just thinking about asking will help. You know someone else who's won out in this kind of problem, so ask what he'd do. List some of the temptations you might be more sure of winning; then you're likely to get a clue to wining this one.

Visualize Your Support

Imagine you can see Satan tempting you, but be sure to look at him through God's eyes. Look at or imagine your favorite picture of Christ, and remember He's watching you *now* with love, involvement, and prayer to God the Father in your behalf. Remember how Christ helped when He was here on earth? He needled, healed, questioned, answered, and understood; from this standpoint, explain this temptation to Him. God commends and rewards the victors; earn His good commendation, now. God limits the devil so that you're never tempted beyond your capacity, so begin with the knowledge you *can* win. Visualize what Jesus would do in your position. Look for the hook in the devil's bait.

Get Moving

Stop staring at the temptation as if you were hypnotized; get a change of air, scenery, different people. Cool the situation by washing your face and hands in cold water, put an ice bag on your neck, or run cold water over your wrists. Go somewhere else; if you can't go physically, move mentally by thinking of other places you'd like to be, things you'd like to do. Go jogging or go for a walk. Sing a song. Change the subject. Count your blessings.

Work out an invention or draw up a sales plan. Think up some suggestions for Christian living under pressure.

Laugh!

Call the devil funny names. Review a good joke or two; poor jokes are better than none for this cause. Think up a one-liner that applies to you, now. Chuckle over how normal and easy this same situation would be if you were surrounded by good people, positive forces for good. Assume your attitude has been wrong and correct it creatively. Figure out a good-humored explanation for your "temporary insanity."

Call on Your Experience

Recall a similar situation, figure out what you should have done then, and go on from there. God never let you down yet, but you haven't always seen that when the pressure was on, of course. He's in there working for you this time, too; so find out what He wants you to do. This temptation is as much a chance for you to discredit the devil as for him to discredit you. Since experience makes you stronger, discredit the devil this time and see that he gets the discredit. Do the *first* right thing you can think of *quickly*.

Learn as Much as You Can

Turn your temptations into opportunities for learning how much you need God. When you lose, ask forgiveness, and read 1 John 1:9–2:2; *accept* the forgiveness God grants. Maybe you can begin to figure out what to look for when the devil attacks next time. If the devil keeps a file on you, why not keep one on him!

Face squarely the simple fact that's so duckable, that you don't always want to win out over your temptations. Being good is often out of style or simply not a status symbol. The temptation battle will continue, for sure; it will require lonely choices, lonely victories, and mistakes will get more publicity than they deserve. At least, it'll seem that way. But your relationship with God is what counts; *He* knows all about that.

10 the God of peace

"The Lord bless you, and watch, guard, and keep you; the Lord make His face to shine upon and enlighten you and be gracious (kind, merciful, and giving favor) to you.

"The Lord lift up His [approving] countenance upon you, and give you peace [tranquility of heart and life continually]." —Numbers 6:24-26, AMP

This beautiful blessing was devised by God Himself at the first use of the tabernacle in the desert. He gave it to the priests to bestow on His own people—people like us.

Jesus Christ is our High Priest. He referred to this same "peace," and expanded it when He said to His disciples, "Peace I leave with you; my [own] peace I now give and bequeath to you. Not as the world gives do I give to you. Do not let your heart be troubled, neither let it be afraid—stop allowing yourselves to be agitated and disturbed; and do not permit yourselves to be fearful and intimidated and cowardly, and unsettled." —John 14:27, AMP